Poetry @ Prayer

Steve Page

Cover Photo by David Travis @ unsplash.com

Copyright © 2023 by Steve Page

This work is licensed under a Creative Commons Attribution-NonCommercial 4.0 International License. You are free to copy and redistribute the material in any medium or format for non-commercial purposes, providing you attribute the work to the author.

First Printing: 2023

ISBN: 9798377323310

Imprint: Independently Published

What?

There's a thin line between prayer and poetry. Look at liturgy for example – surely that's poetry aimed at God. Anyhow, here's a collection of poetry on prayer.

Who?

Steve lives in Ealing and worships at Redeemer London each Sunday at the University of West London. He prays a lot and poets a lot. Sometimes the two meet.

Why?

Steve has a lot of poems lying around, and this is his way of trying to make sense of them. Hopefully they will stir a smile and a prayer.

Why now?

Steve turned 60 last year and has found he prays a whole lot more the older he gets.

Introduction

I'm a pray-er. A lot of us are.

Some are more practiced than others.

Strange thing – I find the more I pray, the more I hear back from God and that prompts me to pray more. It's like a conversation that I never grow tired of and nor does God.

I love it.

That's it.

Simple as that.

Luke 11

One day Jesus was praying in a certain place. When he finished, one of his disciples said to him, *"Lord, teach us to pray…"*

He said to them, *"When you pray, say:*

"Father…"

Our Father

November 2018

We watched and listened as He prayed.
And we wondered what it might be like
to speak with Jehovah as He did.

So we gathered up our courage and we asked.

And then, smiling, He told us.
He gave us our prayer.
And, as if for the first time, it felt real.
It felt like we had permission,
an invitation to call Jehovah 'our Father' as He did.

I couldn't help but smile when I thought
what the priests would make of this.
Child to Father. Direct access. Forgiveness without a priest.
And the simplicity of asking, of feasting
on God's generous Spirit as He did.

Oh, how I smiled. And later, when the others were asleep
I practiced this new boldness and smiled in a whisper:

"Our Father in heaven, most holy be your Name.
Your kingdom come. Your will be done here on earth
just as in heaven.

Give us this day our daily bread. And forgive us our sins
just as we forgive those who sin against us.

And lead us not into temptation,
instead, deliver us from the evil one.

For yours is the kingdom, the power and the glory for ever,
Amen."

I smiled and I slept as He did. Closer to grace.

Luke 11 and Matthew 6

Prayer and response

November 2018

You walk. You sit. You kneel.

You ask. You wait. You weep.

I listen. I speak. I weep.

I hear. I stand. I act.

Strong and Straight

November 2018

Strong knees and open eyes

Straight back and open ears

Strong voice and open hands

Straight through to the throne of grace

Hebrews 4: 14-16

Therefore, since we have a great high priest who has ascended into heaven, Jesus the Son of God, let us hold firmly to the faith we profess. For we do not have a high priest who is unable to empathize with our weaknesses, but we have one who has been tempted in every way, just as we are—yet he did not sin. Let us then approach God's throne of grace with confidence, so that we may receive mercy and find grace to help us in our time of need.

How often do you pray?

November 2018

How many times a day do you pray?

As many as needed.

Some days only once.

But it might take all day.

Praying without listening

November 2018

Have you ever had the feeling

while praying

that you've inadvertently

been talking

while God is speaking?

Don't worry -

He wrote it down for you.

How can I direct your call?

November 2018

Things you won't hear from God:

I'm sorry we are experiencing a higher number of calls than usual.

All of our operators are dealing with other customers.

We will be with you as soon as someone becomes available.

Your call is important to us, please wait or alternatively go to our website.

You may wish to call back later.

Listen carefully to the flowing options.

I'm sorry, I didn't understand that. Did you say, "Help"?

Our office is now closed. Thank you for calling.

Things you will hear from God:

"Welcome. I've been expecting you. What's on your heart?"

Too much

January 2023

When I pray I say too much

and he forgives so much

as his restoring touch

seeps marrow deep

lifting my sorrow

inviting me to rest a while

on both knees

He who loves

October 2022

Hiding prolongs the pain

Running extends the fear

But when you kneel and pray

He who loves comes near

like a mother to a child

like the music in a song

pain and fear will die

you've found where you belong

He is harbour

April 2020

'I hear the Father say,

"Your patience indeed is shallow

- but my restive child, rest and pray,

find in me your refuge,

I am all you need today."

The Lord is harbour. He is anchor.

Once this season passes,

once the channels open

He will be our compass

and we will sail.

A team sport

February 2019

[In the voice of your favourite over-excited rugby commentator.]

"We're inside the final quarter. We've seen a bone-cruncher of a contest today and there's no sign of a let up, the prayers gather for the next engagement, positioning themselves with practiced confidence, skilfully supporting each other, ready for the push. You can see every knee and each hand bears the marks from this long muddied pray, red and brown staining every inch of their entwined limbs; - arms and hands holding fast.

Front row. Second row. Back row.

Digging in for the big push.

The opposition has played an intelligent game, taking advantage of any lapse in concentration, any sign of tiredness, looking for any weakness to exploit. The prayers know they can't afford any slips now, they need to keep up the pressure, maintain their advance deep in the opposition's half. Every yard of gained ground needs to be defended.

The prayers' Coach looks on - look at his smile! You can see the pride he has for his team, he's schooled them on every tactic of the opposition and now that training, that practice has paid dividends.

This is a team of prayers that so clearly know each other well, supporting each other every step of the way. You can see their co-ordinated pray, their sustained effort and the sheer pleasure they feel praying together.

The prayers drive on. The sound of their groans and deep breaths merge into one. There's a rhythm to it, a cadence as together they push and PUSH.

The opposition's footing is slipping, the prayers' momentum gains pace and, YES! the resistance collapses. Oh, that must have hurt!

But there's no time for complacency, the prayers reform their line looking for the next opening, the next opportunity to push forward.

This is a joy to see. The Coach shouts his encouragement - this was never going to be easy struggle; you can't dismiss the opposition - they are a seasoned though sometimes disorganised team and they can take you by surprise. But as we've seen here today, the Coach knows that if his team of prayers keep to the plan and pray to their strengths, the opposition are surely in for a hiding. The prayers will triumph and they will take the winners' crown.

- Back to you in the studio."

Fliers

December 2018

Not everyone flies. You land hard a lot.
Then just as you think it's time for a new direction,
just as you think it's not worth another stumble,
a fresh fall onto your knees,
just then you launch and take flight.

An updraft catches your wings and you're airborne.
And when you eventually land you see that you've got
somewhere new, a whole new perspective.
That's when you know you're a flyer.

Not every line flies. You land hard a lot.
Then just as you think it's time for a new direction,
just as you think it's not worth another stumble,
a fresh fail and an abandoned page,
just then your thoughts take flight.

An updraft catches your wings and you're airborne.
And when you eventually land you see that you've got
somewhere new, a whole new perspective.
That's when you know you're a poet.

Not every prayer flies. You land hard a lot.
Then just as you think it's time for a new direction,
just as you think it's not worth another stumble,
a fresh fall onto your knees,
just then your prayer takes flight.

Your spirit resonates with His and you see His face.
And when you get to your 'Amen', you see that you've got
somewhere new, a whole new perspective.
That's when you know you're a pray-er.

Keep sniffing

March 2017

And when you pray ask from your heart

And when you pray seek from your soul

And when you pray sniff without ceasing

Through your tears to find the doors

That he has prepared for us

That lead to brand new frontiers

For His pioneers.

And then, you knock.

Bedtime

August 2022

I've noticed just how much of our talking waits
until bedtime - as if until then
we have lacked permission to pause
until we've undressed and bundled ourselves
into our duvet time-capsules.

Alas, it's then
when the competing urgency of sleep rises
and meets our log-jammed thoughts

it's then
when our fight fades and our wide meander sprawls,
exhausted of its pungency.

And its then
when our ability to cement thoughts
cracks in the face of creeping sleep
rerunning its classic dreams
and rebuilding forgotten worlds
which we're fated to later abandon
in the shudder of dawn,
and the demands of a new day.

And so, we delay
any conscious introspection
and leave our contemplations to our advancing Sandman
as we slumber and sleepwalk in his wake.

Pentecost

April 2022

My kids, they prophecy daily,
young men recount their visions,
pensioners dream their dreams,
fired up for holy mission.

I wonder about those like me
caught in our middle-ages.
What did Joel have in mind
for men in mid-life crises?

God tells me I'm still chosen,
I still do qualify
to bear ripe fruit, to share good gifts,
to live without compromise.

So as the last days come much nearer,
as our mission nears completion,
you'll find I pray more readily
to herald his coming kingdom.

Acts 2:17-18 quotes the prophet Joel:
"In the last days, God says, I will pour out my Spirit on all people. Your sons and daughters will prophesy, your young men will see visions, your old men will dream dreams. Even on my servants, both men and women, I will pour out my Spirit in those days, and they will prophesy."

Practice

April 2022

If you want to learn to play the guitar, you find a tutorial book, you learn the chords, the rhythms, the techniques and you practice, practice, practice. Sometimes its hard work. More often it's fun.

If you want to write songs, you write. Some are just play, with no real meaning; some songs express your heart. Both are worthwhile. Some sound good and connect with others. Some don't. That's fine.

If you stop playing, if you stop writing you will get rusty. But you can pick it up again.

Poetry is the same. Keep writing.

Prayer is the same too. Keep talking.

Handrail

March 2022

Prayer, like poetry can hand me
a handrail for the steps down,
can steady me for the unexplored depths.

Prayer can hand me confidence
that I am not alone
that there are words
gifting markers of hope
leading me back to the surface
should I choose it.

Lesson

March 2022

The first lesson is to be still
the next is to wait
while you look long and listen deep
that you might love all the more.

'There's only one lesson in painting, and that is to look."
Louis Wain.
In life, in prayer, the lesson is similar.

Think on these things

September 2021

I think on what is true and just and honourable
I think on what is pure and lovely and admirable
I consider what is excellent and what is praiseworthy
and I praise our God who is unmistakably
the creator of all of these and more -

I think on what is true.

I think of God's voice, his true promise,
his true plumbline, directing the eye down
to the centre, a reliable reference,
an alignment to righteousness.
I see the weight, suspended
and I wait as it finds the true vertical axis
pointing to the centre of gravity
as if that was its true purpose all along
- not to gravitate us down, but to re-direct us
to a true line upon which we can centre ourselves.

I think on what is true.

I think on what is honourable, noble.

I think of honour lists and of inherited nobility,
I think of integrity, living up to the responsibility
of my privilege and authority
and of using it responsibly, with generosity,

recognising opportunities to live
nobly, dependably
ethically, reliably,
faithful to the One who entrusted me
with so much extraordinary bounty.

I think on what is honourable.

I think on what is just and right.

I think about the courage to live fully in the light,
to stand up for what we know to be the right
to admit to ourselves when we don't get it right
to give heart-felt apology, to find a way to re-unite,
to fight injustice alongside those who can't
to go the extra mile when our heads say don't.

Not doing what they'd do to you
if the tables were turned,
but doing what you'd have them do
if the circumstances were reversed

And when the right of it still isn't clear
to wait and figure it out, take the longer route
rather than the obvious, shorter cut
and if, even then, you can't be sure
err on the side of the generous cut
because we know that the Cross wasn't fair
but it was right and it was just.

I think on what is right.

I think on what is pure.

I think about the sudden clarity of a cold mountain stream
bubbling up from its spring,
running through and digging down irrespective of obstacles
flowing over all rocky hurdles
with pure, unadulterated intent
to get at last to the sea
where its creator intended it to be.

I think on what is pure.

I think on what is lovely.

I think of the surface-beauty that catches my eye
but then of the beauty that only shows itself in the depths
- in patience, in the willingness
to put ill-feeling to rest
and to embrace forgiveness
and thereby release a smile that meets
that generous high-beauty in full gratefulness.

I think on what is lovely.

I think on what is admirable, commendable
and of good reputation,
and I think how God views me is more important
than the admiration offered by others.
I think that what is commendable
is in the eye of the beholder
and that my Beholder sees the heart
and so I entrust my reputation to the One who sees better.

I think on what is admirable.

I think on what is excellent
and I think past Bill and Ted to something
of diamond quality,
of designed symmetry,
of clarity, of weight
or perhaps of a line in a poem or a song,
something that takes away my breath.

But then I see the sun through trees,
shining on breakfasting friends
and on my laughter
and I think that this is truly God's most excellent.

I think on what is praiseworthy.

I think of the ovation given to a practiced orchestra
and pitch perfect soloists
and then I think of a five-year-old niece
mastering her first recorder
and getting to that tricky last line of
Twinkle Twinkle Little Star
and I think, for our God,
this effort, this success is by far
most praiseworthy.

We think on what is true and just and honourable
we think on what is pure and lovely and admirable
we consider what is excellent and what is praiseworthy
and we praise our God who is unmistakably
the creator of all of these and more.

And I think that perhaps we too
are a little lovely and that we too
are partially admirable
and I think perhaps we too
are not a little praiseworthy.

And so when I think on these things,
I think on you, on us,
and I praise our God all the more.

Think on these things.

Philippians 4:8
"...whatever is true, whatever is honorable, whatever is just, whatever is pure, whatever is lovely, whatever is commendable, if there is any excellence, if there is anything worthy of praise, think about these things."

Habakkuk Joy

July 2021

I will take joy in my sadness
I will make praise in my complaint
I will walk tall as I stumble
And stand firm even as I faint

I see death rise around me
sickness renews its attack
But while you remain my saviour
There's nothing that I lack

You're the light in my cold darkness
You're the song in my despair
You're the peace in this chaos
You're the answer to my prayer

So I'll confess my allegiance
I will shout your name with pride
I will take joy in my salvation
and climb with you, my guide

Habakkuk 3.18-19
" - I will take joy in the God of my salvation, God the Lord is my strength; he makes my feet like the deer's; he makes me tread on my high places."–

Double touch

February 2020

Come - and take a double touch of His grace
on your tear stained face,
hinging on His mercy
coupled with His ability
to not assume, to not barrel past,
but to rather ask (and twice ask)
with a balm of a voice and intentional hearing
and His long compassionate waiting.

Come - and take a double touch of His grace,

Jesus wasn't one for placing His touch 'in passing',
but He placed His touch with presence -
His presence was off-the-fence, no-pretence full in the face.

Come - and take a double touch of His grace,

He held back from the passing pack
and exercised the knack of knowing to look back,
going far enough to reach a truer understanding,
to reach out with both arms and so allowing
Him to encompass all previous experience
of others heavy handed mishandling.

Come - and take a double touch of His grace.

For He knows that truthfully the healing is secondary
to the placing of a true medicinal touch,
to the reassuring brush of acceptance,

to the knowing that you've received close hearing
and been held with a closer grasping -
a meeting of more than minds,
a confidence of souls truly entwined,
standing embracing and only releasing
once we have the assurance of knowing
that we've been double-touched with honesty
and that we're twice as much connected fully
and gracefully with the One who truly
never turned from anyone's face.

Come - and take a double touch of His grace.

Mark 8:22-25
They came to Bethsaida, and some people brought a blind man and begged Jesus to touch him. He took the blind man by the hand and led him outside the village. When he had spit on the man's eyes and put his hands on him, Jesus asked, "Do you see anything?" He looked up and said, "I see people; they look like trees walking around." Once more Jesus put his hands on the man's eyes. Then his eyes were opened, his sight was restored, and he saw everything clearly.

Mary-ing

February 2020

Each day I pray for an ear that will hear
above all the noise clearly His voice.

For while sometimes it's best to be serving with zest,
sometimes it's better to sit for a breather

and wait in his presence and enjoy this true essence
of sitting and being before going and doing.

So, while sometimes I'll Martha I know that I'd rather
spend time being Mary, in less of a hurry,

for there at his feet I'll be that more complete
and hear his clear voice above all the noise.

Today - where can I mary and where can I martha?
There's time for them both,
but I know which is better.

Go to Luke 10 for the original account.

The jazz

January 2020

And where do you keep the jazz?
Where do you store the melancholy,
the self-reflection and the escape.

Direct me to the place you keep
for your inner, your deeper,
your best kept back

and let's sit and explore,
let's jazz and coalesce into a more honest
and more innovative
improv.

Sparked by a scene from a novel 'Moon over Soho' by Ben Aaronovitch.

Treacle

December 2019

Time here is treacle –

it's thick and syrupy, a rich golden glow
that envelopes the spoon while flowing
over the edges inevitably leaving a trail, a thread if you will,
that will never be chased down or scooped up without leaving
a sticky sweet trace that will last days
before it fully fades
to a savoured memory.

Time here is golden treacle.

Reflection

November 2019

I sat in front of the mirror and reflected on age and plans and paths and happenstance. And as I reflected, my reflection faded and I looked onward and found a new road, a narrower path and an older way, leading me to my paths-maker rather than to my path-dictator and to my next choice on the adventure that my maker had made free and had made ordained, one and the same.

And as I looked, the dark fell, and the light rose and reflected well on our choice. And so, I too rose, and we walked on.

Proverbs 2:20
Thus you will walk in the ways of the good and keep to the paths of the righteous.
Proverbs 27:19
As water reflects the face, so one's life reflects the heart. (and so others reflect your heart back to you.)
1 Corinthians 13:12
For now we see only a reflection as in a mirror; then we shall see face to face. Now I know in part; then I shall know fully, even as I am fully known.
Acts 2:28
You have made known to me the paths of life; you will fill me with joy in your presence.'

Where is your Orkney?

August 2019

Where have you found your Orkney?
Where do you find you're centred?
Where would you say your true self is?
Where can you best be remembered?

Is it in a familiar voice? Is it in a sound?
Is it in a childhood smell or is it more place-bound?

Is it when you're free to dance
or when you get up to sing?
When you pick up a favourite pen
and your mind has taken wing?

Is it as you walk or stroll or in the pace of a run?
Is it when you find your chill or when you're having fun?

Is it when you're home alone
or when you're there with others?
Is it found when standing solo
or within greater numbers?

Where is your Orkney? Where are you centred?
Wherever it is where your true self is - go there, meet God
and remember.

The title is from a radio conversation about mental health and the place art has in preserving it. But I wondered about prayer.

Before the memory fades

August 2019

Ask now about the former days,
ask before praying
before this pause
passes.

Listen now about the former days,
listen before rising
before this story
ends.

Speak now about the former days,
speak before forgetting
before this memory
fades.

Prompted by this quote from Deuteronomy 4: 32.
'Place value on what has gone before. Ask now about the former days, long before your time, from the day God created human beings on the earth; ask from one end of the heavens to the other. Has anything so great as this ever happened, or has anything like it ever been heard of?"

Faith

April 2019

The certainty that gives

the clarity to see

a path lies beneath

the current uncertainty

More

July 2019

Believe in more than you can imagine
Believe in more than you ask to happen
Believe in more than what you have seen
Believe in more than what you have been
Believe in more than your faded label
Believe in more cos your God is able.

Immeasurably more than all we ask
Immeasurably more than all we imagine
Immeasurably more than what we deserve
Immeasurably more than mere human passions.

Immeasurably wider
Immeasurably longer
Immeasurably higher
Immeasurably deeper
Immeasurably more - full to the brim
Immeasurable love to the fulness of Him.

Ephesians 3:20-21
Now to him who is able to do immeasurably more than all we ask or imagine, according to his power that is at work within us, to him be glory in the church and in Christ Jesus throughout all generations, for ever and ever! Amen.

Psalm 33 Plus

July 2019

It is fitting to praise you with joyful song.
It is fitting to make stringed music to you.
It is fitting to sing new songs to you,
to play skilfully to you and to shout joyfully to you,
our God and Maker.

It is fitting to hope in your unfailing love,
to hope in your help and in your shield
to hope in your fearful, unfailing love,
our God and King.

It is fitting to praise you in the kitchen
with spoon and saucepan
with smart speaker on full volume.

It is fitting for the family to worship you
with loud bellows in the car,
with all the windows down.

It is fitting to praise you in the congregation,
in the Town Hall, in the parks and in the university,
in places of further wisdom your people praise you.

It is fitting to play skilfully to you
to play with drums and cymbals.

Q & A

June 2019

Jesus didn't hand you solutions.
Jesus didn't give you your answers.
Jesus asked YOU the questions.
Jesus was and is your answer.

He is the Way the Truth the Life.
He is the River the Bread the Light.
He is the Shepherd the Gate the Vine.
He is Human. He is Divine.

He is the Lamb. He is the Lion.
He is the Word and He's not lyin'.
He is the Servant. He is the Prince.
He is Love and I am convinced

Jesus came to seek and to save.
Bigger than a manger. Stronger than the grave.
Jesus came as God made man...

He - asked - you - a - question -
"What about YOU?
Who do YOU say I am?"

Written for a music and spoken word event (Cafe Church @ St Johns, Ealing) on the theme of Questions. Luke 9.20

Also from Steve Page

If you enjoyed this collection, you just might enjoy

Not Too Big To Weep;

Not Too Old To Dance;

Not Too Soon For Christmas;

Father is a Verb;

Fruity Poetry;

Wisdom Poetry

Real Christmas Poetry; and

Hollow Egg. Empty Grave.

If you still want more, you can find me amongst a world-wide crowd of poets on https://hellopoetry.com

And if you're into prose try:

Deborah's Daughter; and

A man walks into a bar.

Printed in Great Britain
by Amazon